GARY CHAPMAN
RAMON PRESSON

# Love Talks

## FOR FAMILIES

*101 Questions to Stimulate Interaction with Your Family*

NORTHFIELD PUBLISHING
CHICAGO

Entry #43 first appeared in Ramon Presson, *Stress Busters* (Littleton: Colo.: Serendipity House, 2001). Used by permission.

Gary Chapman Photo: David Smith

ISBN: 978-1-881273-49-3

9 11 13 14 12 10

*Printed in the United States of America*

## *Tips for Using Love Talks for Families*

One of the signs of a healthy family is open and meaningful communication. Good questions are the beginning. Here are some ways to use the questions:

- During dinner at home
- During a quiet moment in the evening
- Just before bedtime
- While in the car during a long drive
- On vacations

Parents, introduce the idea to your children and teens by describing this product as a game. Don't sell it as some serious communication project your family is going to do. Note that the questions are designed to interest most school age children and teenagers.

Therefore, every question encourages participation from every family member.

Parents may want to secure agreement upon a few ground rules:

- If you don't want to answer a question, you don't have to.
- If you can't think of an answer at the moment, your response will certainly be welcome at a later time.
- When someone is sharing an answer, everyone else will listen attentively without interrupting.
- All genuine responses will be respected and affirmed.

While the easiest way to proceed through the questions is to use them in the order they are presented, another possibility is to allow family members to take turns in selecting the questions. We recommend that you do only one or two questions at a time. And don't do them

every day. Make your children ask for more, not less. These questions are like dessert—a small and satisfying portion creates the anticipation for more later.

*Love Talks for Families* is great for single-parent and blended families as well. Have fun with these questions a few times a week and enjoy the improved family communication.

*Give each member of the family
an imaginary award for an achievement
or something special they did recently.*

Love Talks

FOR FAMILIES

*Give each member of the family an imaginary award for an achievement or something special they did recently.*

# *Name one talent you wish you had.*

*Name one talent you wish you had.*

Love Talks
FOR FAMILIES

*If you had to give up sight, hearing,*

*the ability to speak, or the ability to walk,*

*which would you choose?*

Love Talks

FOR FAMILIES

*If* you had to give up sight, hearing,
the ability to speak, or the ability to walk,
which would you choose?

Love Talks
FOR FAMILIES

*If you had a magic wand
and could change anything in your life
right now, what would it be?*

Love Talks
FOR FAMILIES

*If you had a magic wand
and could change anything in your life
right now, what would it be?*

Love Talks
FOR FAMILIES

*If you could be on any magazine cover,*

*which one would you select?*

Love Talks

FOR FAMILIES

*If you could be on any magazine cover,*

*which one would you select?*

Love Talks
FOR FAMILIES

*If you could go on a vacation to another country,*

*which one would you select?*

Love Talks

FOR FAMILIES

— QUESTION 6 —

*If you could go on a vacation to another country,*

*which one would you select?*

Love Talks
FOR FAMILIES

*What is one of your favorite stories that your parent(s) tell about you?*

Love Talks
FOR FAMILIES

*What is one of your favorite stories that your parent(s) tell about you?*

Love Talks
FOR FAMILIES

*If we had to move from our home
to another city, what would you miss the most
about our home? Our neighborhood? Our city?
Whom would you miss the most?*

Love Talks
FOR FAMILIES

*If* we had to move from our home
to another city, what would you miss the most
about our home? Our neighborhood? Our city?
Whom would you miss the most?

Love Talks
FOR FAMILIES

*If you could have any kind of unconventional pet,*

*what would you choose?*

Love Talks
FOR FAMILIES

*If you could have any kind of unconventional pet,*

*what would you choose?*

Love Talks

FOR FAMILIES

*What is the best reason you can think of*

*not to use alcohol or drugs?*

Love Talks

FOR FAMILIES

*What is the best reason you can think of*

*not to use alcohol or drugs?*

Love Talks
FOR FAMILIES

*B*estow a "Fruit of the Spirit Award" *(Galatians 5:22-23)*
upon each family member. From the following,
affirm the quality you observed recently.

☐ *love*          ☐ *joy*          ☐ *peace*

☐ *patience*      ☐ *goodness*     ☐ *faithfulness*

☐ *gentleness*    ☐ *kindness*     ☐ *self-control*

Love Talks
FOR FAMILIES

*Bestow a "Fruit of the Spirit Award" (Galatians 5:22-23)*
*upon each family member. From the following,*
*affirm the quality you observed recently.*

☐ *love*　　　　☐ *joy*　　　　☐ *peace*

☐ *patience*　　☐ *goodness*　　☐ *faithfulness*

☐ *gentleness*　☐ *kindness*　　☐ *self-control*

Love Talks
FOR FAMILIES

— QUESTION 12 —

*What dessert do you think*

*you could eat for a lifetime?*

Love Talks
FOR FAMILIES

*What dessert do you think you could eat for a lifetime?*

Love Talks
FOR FAMILIES

*In Acts 12 young Rhoda told the people*

*in the house that Peter was knocking on the door,*

*but they didn't believe her.*

*Can you recall a time that you were*

*telling the truth but someone didn't believe you?*

Love Talks
FOR FAMILIES

*In Acts 12 young Rhoda told the people
in the house that Peter was knocking on the door,
but they didn't believe her.
Can you recall a time that you were
telling the truth but someone didn't believe you?*

Love Talks
FOR FAMILIES

*If you could ask God any question,*

*what would you ask?*

*If you could ask God any question,*

*what would you ask?*

Love Talks

FOR FAMILIES

*T*alk about a time when it felt good to help someone.

*L*ove *T*alks
FOR FAMILIES

*Talk about a time when it felt good to help someone.*

Love Talks
FOR FAMILIES

*If I could be any kind of animal for a day,*

*I'd like to be a . . .*

Love Talks

FOR FAMILIES

*If I could be any kind of animal for a day,*

*I'd like to be a . . .*

Love Talks
FOR FAMILIES

# Which of the following would you like to have in your backyard?

- [ ] go-cart track
- [ ] miniature golf course
- [ ] underground headquarters
- [ ] treehouse

- [ ] swimming pool
- [ ] tennis court
- [ ] 20 pieces of playground equipment
- [ ] other: _____

- [ ] greenhouse
- [ ] clubhouse

Love Talks
FOR FAMILIES

## *W*hich of the following would you like to have in your backyard?

☐ go-cart track  ☐ swimming pool  ☐ greenhouse

☐ miniature golf course  ☐ tennis court  ☐ clubhouse

☐ underground headquarters  ☐ 20 pieces of playground equipment

☐ treehouse  ☐ other: _____

Love Talks
FOR FAMILIES

*I*n the **Chronicles of Narnia,** *four children walked through a wardrobe (clothes) closet and into the magical land of Narnia. If you had a magic door in the back of your closet that could take you to one special place anytime you want to go, where would it be?*

*L*ove *T*alks
FOR FAMILIES

*In* the **Chronicles of Narnia,** *four children*
*walked through a wardrobe (clothes) closet*
*and into the magical land of Narnia.*
*If you had a magic door in the back of your closet*
*that could take you to one special place anytime*
*you want to go, where would it be?*

Love Talks
FOR FAMILIES

— QUESTION 19 —

*What is something that would be hard for you to share?*

Love Talks
FOR FAMILIES

— QUESTION 19 —

*What is something that would be hard for you to share?*

— QUESTION 20 —

*As a surprise for your birthday we've arranged for a famous person of your choice to attend. Whom will you choose?*

Love Talks

FOR FAMILIES

*As a surprise for your birthday we've arranged*
*for a famous person of your choice*
*to attend. Whom will you choose?*

Love Talks
FOR FAMILIES

*I wish I had a personal coach, tutor, or mentor for . . .*

Love Talks
FOR FAMILIES

*I wish I had a personal coach, tutor, or mentor for . . .*

— QUESTION 22 —

*What is one of the most uninteresting things*

*you have to do on a regular basis?*

Love Talks
FOR FAMILIES

– QUESTION 22 –

*What is one of the most uninteresting things*

*you have to do on a regular basis?*

Love Talks
FOR FAMILIES

*Using the first letter of your first name, the family must come up with a positive word that begins with the same letter to describe you. For example: Talented Trevor or Generous Ginny.*

Love Talks
FOR FAMILIES

*Using the first letter of your first name, the family must come up with a positive word that begins with the same letter to describe you. For example: Talented Trevor or Generous Ginny.*

Love Talks
FOR FAMILIES

*What were the best and worst moments*

*from this past week?*

*Love Talks*

FOR FAMILIES

*What were the best and worst moments from this past week?*

Love Talks

FOR FAMILIES

*In what Olympic sports event would you like*

*to win a gold medal?*

*In what Olympic sports event would you like*

*to win a gold medal?*

*Everyone has five minutes to scout the house for objects that positively describe members of the family, then use the object in a sentence to describe the person. For example: "I have a light bulb for Cameron because he brings light into our house"; or "I have a paper clip for Mom because she holds our family together."*

Love Talks
FOR FAMILIES

*Everyone has five minutes to scout the house for objects that positively describe members of the family, then use the object in a sentence to describe the person. For example: "I have a light bulb for Cameron because he brings light into our house"; or "I have a paper clip for Mom because she holds our family together."*

Love Talks
FOR FAMILIES

*This week my internal weather could be described as:*

☐ *partly cloudy*    ☐ *partly sunny*

☐ *hot and dry*    ☐ *unpredictable thunderstorms*

☐ *cold and rainy*    ☐ *early fog, then clearing*

☐ *frost warning*    ☐ *Other: _____*

Love Talks
FOR FAMILIES

*T*his week my internal weather could be described as:

- ☐ *partly cloudy*
- ☐ *partly sunny*
- ☐ *hot and dry*
- ☐ *unpredictable thunderstorms*
- ☐ *cold and rainy*
- ☐ *early fog, then clearing*
- ☐ *frost warning*
- ☐ *Other:* _____

*L*ove *T*alks
FOR FAMILIES

*If at the end of every day you were granted*

*an extra hour to do anything you wanted,*

*how would you regularly spend that hour?*

Love Talks
FOR FAMILIES

*If at the end of every day you were granted an extra hour to do anything you wanted, how would you regularly spend that hour?*

Love Talks
FOR FAMILIES

*Tell family members about a compliment
or affirmation that you've received recently
from someone outside the family.*

*Tell family members about a compliment or affirmation that you've received recently from someone outside the family.*

*Who is someone in our extended family (grandparent, aunt, uncle, cousin, in-law) that you wish you could spend more time with?*

Love Talks
FOR FAMILIES

*Who is someone in our extended family (grandparent, aunt, uncle, cousin, in-law) that you wish you could spend more time with?*

Love Talks

FOR FAMILIES

$\mathcal{G}$ive each member of the family an imaginary
gift certificate to a favorite store, for a favorite
or wished-for product or special event.

Love Talks
FOR FAMILIES

*Give each member of the family an imaginary gift certificate to a favorite store, for a favorite or wished-for product or special event.*

Love Talks

FOR FAMILIES

*Who is someone in our extended family, neighborhood, school, church, or workplace for whom we could do something helpful? What could we do?*

Love Talks
FOR FAMILIES

*Who is someone in our extended family,*

*neighborhood, school, church, or workplace*

*for whom we could do something helpful?*

*What could we do?*

Love Talks

FOR FAMILIES

*About bullies*

CHILDREN: *Who is the biggest bully at your school?*

PARENTS: *Recall a bully at your school.*

BOTH: *Why do you think some kids become mean?*

*Love Talks*
FOR FAMILIES

# *A*bout bullies

CHILDREN: *Who is the biggest bully at your school?*

PARENTS: *Recall a bully at your school.*

BOTH: *Why do you think some kids become mean?*

*L*ove *T*alks
FOR FAMILIES

*About trading places*

CHILDREN: *I think the best part about being*

*a grown-up would be . . .*

PARENTS: *I think the best part about being a kid*

*again would be . . .*

*Love Talks*

FOR FAMILIES

*A*bout trading places

CHILDREN: *I think the best part about being a grown-up would be . . .*

PARENTS: *I think the best part about being a kid again would be . . .*

Love Talks
FOR FAMILIES

*The Early Years*

PARENTS: *Recall and describe some special detail*
*or feeling you remember about the day*
*each child was born or adopted.*

CHILDREN: *What is your earliest childhood*
*memory (one of the first that comes to mind)?*

Love Talks
FOR FAMILIES

*The Early Years*

PARENTS: *Recall and describe some special detail*

*or feeling you remember about the day*

*each child was born or adopted.*

CHILDREN: *What is your earliest childhood*

*memory (one of the first that comes to mind)?*

Love Talks

FOR FAMILIES

*If you were President of the United States for a day, who is someone that you would honor with a special award?*

Love Talks
FOR FAMILIES

*If you were President of the United States*

*for a day, who is someone that you*

*would honor with a special award?*

Love Talks

FOR FAMILIES

*What is your favorite television commercial?*

Love Talks

FOR FAMILIES

*What is your favorite television commercial?*

*If you could change anything*

*about your appearance, what would you change?*

Love Talks
FOR FAMILIES

*If you could change anything*

*about your appearance, what would you change?*

*Love Talks*

FOR FAMILIES

*What is your favorite time of the day?*

*Favorite day of the week?*

*Favorite month of the year?*

*What is your favorite time of the day?*

*Favorite day of the week?*

*Favorite month of the year?*

Love Talks
FOR FAMILIES

*Recall a family outing or vacation that went badly*

*but you're able to laugh about now.*

Love Talks

FOR FAMILIES

*Recall a family outing or vacation that went badly but you're able to laugh about now.*

*Complete this sentence:*

*"I feel especially close to you when . . ."*

*Love Talks*
FOR FAMILIES

*Complete this sentence:*

*"I feel especially close to you when . . ."*

– QUESTION 42 –

*What was your best day this past week?*

– QUESTION 42 –

*What was your best day this past week?*

Love Talks
FOR FAMILIES

# *What animal best illustrates how you deal with conflict?*

☐ lion—attack first

☐ bird—fly away

☐ snake—attack if provoked

☐ peacock—make a scene

☐ turtle—turn inward and silent

☐ skunk—fight dirty

☐ puppy—whimper and cry

☐ other _____

Love Talks

FOR FAMILIES

## *What* animal best illustrates how you deal with conflict?

- ☐ lion—attack first
- ☐ bird—fly away
- ☐ snake—attack if provoked
- ☐ peacock—make a scene

- ☐ turtle—turn inward and silent
- ☐ skunk—fight dirty
- ☐ puppy—whimper and cry
- ☐ other _____

Love Talks
FOR FAMILIES

*P*ARENTS: *A rule that I wish we had in my family*

*growing up is . . .*

CHILDREN: *A rule in our family I wish*

*I could change is . . .*

*L*ove *T*alks

FOR FAMILIES

*P*ARENTS: *A rule that I wish we had in my family*

*growing up is . . .*

CHILDREN: *A rule in our family I wish*

*I could change is . . .*

*L*ove *T*alks
FOR FAMILIES

— QUESTION 45 —

*Talk about a time you were scared.*

Love Talks
FOR FAMILIES

– QUESTION 45 –

*Talk about a time you were scared.*

Love Talks
FOR FAMILIES

*Conflict is rather normal in all families.*
*Forgiveness is a gift regularly offered in healthy*
*families. Complete the following sentence:*
*"(Name), I'm glad you're not still angry*
*at me for . . ."*

*Love Talks*
FOR FAMILIES

*Conflict is rather normal in all families.*
*Forgiveness is a gift regularly offered in healthy*
*families. Complete the following sentence:*
*"(Name), I'm glad you're not still angry*
*at me for . . ."*

Love Talks
FOR FAMILIES

— QUESTION 47—

*Recall a time when someone
(not a family member) hurt your feelings.*

Love Talks
FOR FAMILIES

*Recall a time when someone
(not a family member) hurt your feelings.*

Love Talks
FOR FAMILIES

*Recall a time when you were nervous about having to do something in front of a lot of people (recitation, give a report or speech, sing, play an instrument, play a sport, etc.).*

*R*ecall a time when you were nervous about having
to do something in front of a lot of people
(recitation, give a report or speech, sing,
play an instrument, play a sport, etc.).

Love Talks
FOR FAMILIES

*Recall a time that you were really embarrassed.*

*Recall a time that you were really embarrassed.*

*Complete this sentence: "I wish I had the (courage, time, or money) to try . . ."*

*Love Talks*
FOR FAMILIES

*C*omplete this sentence: *"I wish I had the (courage, time, or money) to try . . ."*

Love Talks
FOR FAMILIES

*Recently I didn't feel very pleased with myself*

*when I . . .*

*Recently I didn't feel very pleased with myself*

*when I . . .*

Love Talks
FOR FAMILIES

*Each person comes up with a separate*

*answer for every family member:*

*"I know that something that drives you nuts is . . ."*

*Love Talks*

FOR FAMILIES

*Each person comes up with a separate*

*answer for every family member:*

*"I know that something that drives you nuts is . . ."*

Love Talks
FOR FAMILIES

*How much influence do you think your friends have on you?*

*How much influence do you think your friends have on you?*

Love Talks
FOR FAMILIES

*If* the Fruit of the Spirit (Galatians 5:22-23)
grew on trees, which one would you most want
to plant in our yard for yourself?

☐ *love*  ☐ *joy*  ☐ *peace*

☐ *patience*  ☐ *goodness*  ☐ *faithfulness*

☐ *gentleness*  ☐ *kindness*  ☐ *self-control*

Love Talks
FOR FAMILIES

*If the Fruit of the Spirit (Galatians 5:22–23) grew on trees, which one would you most want to plant in our yard for yourself?*

☐ *love*  ☐ *joy*  ☐ *peace*

☐ *patience*  ☐ *goodness*  ☐ *faithfulness*

☐ *gentleness*  ☐ *kindness*  ☐ *self-control*

Love Talks
FOR FAMILIES

*What is something that you are worried about
these days (or typically worry about)?*

Love Talks
FOR FAMILIES

*What is something that you are worried about these days (or typically worry about)?*

Love Talks
FOR FAMILIES

*Tell about a time you felt very sad.*

*Tell about a time you felt very sad.*

Love Talks
FOR FAMILIES

*Each person has a love language, a way in which they feel truly loved. What do you think is the love language of each person in our family?*

☐ *Physical touch (hugs, kisses, cuddling)*

☐ *Words of affirmation ("I love you," "I missed you today," "You look great").*

☐ *Acts of service (doing something special to help or surprise)*

☐ *Quality time (spending time together in a way that is meaningful for the other)*

☐ *Receiving gifts (tokens of love; items the person likes or enjoys)*

Love Talks
FOR FAMILIES

*Each person has a love language, a way in which they feel truly loved. What do you think is the love language of each person in our family?*

☐ *Physical touch (hugs, kisses, cuddling)*

☐ *Words of affirmation ("I love you," "I missed you today," "You look great").*

☐ *Acts of service (doing something special to help or surprise)*

☐ *Quality time (spending time together in a way that is meaningful for the other)*

☐ *Receiving gifts (tokens of love; items the person likes or enjoys)*

Love Talks
FOR FAMILIES

*One of the things that I like most about*

*our church (or community) is . . .*

*Love Talks*

FOR FAMILIES

*One of the things that I like most about*

*our church (or community) is . . .*

*Love Talks*

FOR FAMILIES

*Recall a family experience involving one of the following: fishing, hunting, biking, hiking, or camping.*

*Recall a family experience involving one of the following: fishing, hunting, biking, hiking, or camping.*

*The* lion, otter, beaver, and golden retriever

are animals used to describe four personality types.

Which one do you think best describes you?

☐ *I'm a lion: strong, confident, a leader; I like to make sure things get done.*

☐ *I'm an otter: very outgoing, humorous, creative. I enjoy people.*

☐ *I'm a beaver: detail-oriented and organized. I follow instructions and am good with projects.*

☐ *I'm a golden retriever: loyal, sensitive, caring.*

Love Talks

FOR FAMILIES

*The lion, otter, beaver, and golden retriever
are animals used to describe four personality types.
Which one do you think best describes you?*

☐ *I'm a lion: strong, confident,
a leader; I like to make sure
things get done.*

☐ *I'm an otter: very outgoing,
humorous, creative. I enjoy
people.*

☐ *I'm a beaver: detail-oriented and
organized. I follow instructions
and am good with projects.*

☐ *I'm a golden retriever: loyal,
sensitive, caring.*

Love Talks
FOR FAMILIES

*Recall a family memory involving
one of the following:*

☐ zoo ☐ theme park ☐ sporting event

☐ playground ☐ carnival ☐ circus

*Recall a family memory involving
one of the following:*

☐ zoo      ☐ theme park      ☐ sporting event

☐ playground      ☐ carnival      ☐ circus

Love Talks
FOR FAMILIES

*Recall a funny family time involving one of the following:*

☐ *fresh snow*

☐ *slick ice*

☐ *beach sand*

☐ *fall leaves*

☐ *gloppy mud*

Love Talks
FOR FAMILIES

*Recall a funny family time involving one of the following:*

☐ *fresh snow*

☐ *slick ice*

☐ *beach sand*

☐ *fall leaves*

☐ *gloppy mud*

Love Talks
FOR FAMILIES

*Describe two things that happened today and how you felt about each of them.*

Love Talks
FOR FAMILIES

*Describe two things that happened today and how you felt about each of them.*

Love Talks
FOR FAMILIES

# *R*ecall a family moment
## at one of the following:

☐ *ocean*  ☐ *creek*

☐ *lake*  ☐ *mountain stream*

☐ *pond*  ☐ *waterfall*

☐ *river*

*Love Talks*
FOR FAMILIES

# *R*ecall a family moment
## at one of the following:

- ☐ ocean
- ☐ lake
- ☐ pond
- ☐ river
- ☐ creek
- ☐ mountain stream
- ☐ waterfall

*Love Talks*
FOR FAMILIES

*I think the best job in the world would be . . .*

*I think the best job in the world would be . . .*

*CHILDREN: What is your favorite toy?*

*What is your favorite candy?*

PARENTS: *What were some of your favorite toys?*

*Some of your favorite candy?*

Love Talks
FOR FAMILIES

CHILDREN: *What is your favorite toy?*

*What is your favorite candy?*

PARENTS: *What were some of your favorite toys?*

*Some of your favorite candy?*

Love Talks
FOR FAMILIES

# You remind me of

☐ *Jesus the Healer*

☐ *Jesus the Servant*

☐ *Jesus the Preacher*

☐ *Jesus the Storyteller*

☐ *Jesus the Revolutionary*

Love Talks
FOR FAMILIES

*You remind me of*

☐ *Jesus the Healer*

☐ *Jesus the Servant*

☐ *Jesus the Preacher*

☐ *Jesus the Storyteller*

☐ *Jesus the Revolutionary*

Love Talks
FOR FAMILIES

*Our family has been invited to join the Ringling Brothers, Barnum & Bailey Circus. What role will you perform? Which would you least like to do?*

Love Talks
FOR FAMILIES

*Our family has been invited to join the Ringling Brothers, Barnum & Bailey Circus. What role will you perform? Which would you least like to do?*

*— QUESTION 69 —*

# *Recall a family experience involving one of the following:*

☐ *a bike ride*  ☐ *a train ride*

☐ *a boat ride*  ☐ *a carnival ride*

☐ *a plane ride*

Love Talks
FOR FAMILIES

*Recall a family experience involving one of the following:*

☐ a bike ride ☐ a train ride

☐ a boat ride ☐ a carnival ride

☐ a plane ride

*When have you felt like an outsider—*

*like you weren't part of the group?*

Love Talks

FOR FAMILIES

*When have you felt like an outsider—like you weren't part of the group?*

*O*ne of television's most popular game shows was
Let's Make a Deal, *offering the risk of gain
and loss. If Monty Hall, the host, were to say
to you,* "You can keep the $3,000 or trade it
for what's behind the curtain," *what would you do?*

*L*ove *T*alks
FOR FAMILIES

*O*ne *of television's most popular game shows was*
Let's Make a Deal, *offering the risk of gain*
*and loss. If Monty Hall, the host, were to say*
*to you, "You can keep the $3,000 or trade it*
*for what's behind the curtain," what would you do?*

Love Talks
FOR FAMILIES

*What is something in nature (plants, animals,*

*fish, geography, weather, space, etc.) that*

*truly fascinates you?*

*What is something in nature (plants, animals, fish, geography, weather, space, etc.) that truly fascinates you?*

*Of whom would you like to have*

*an autographed photo?*

*Of whom would you like to have*

*an autographed photo?*

Love Talks
FOR FAMILIES

*Each person is to flip a coin*

*and answer the appropriate question below.*

HEADS: *What was something encouraging*

*or positive that happened today?*

TAILS: *What was something disappointing*

*or difficult that happened today?*

*Love Talks*

FOR FAMILIES

*Each person is to flip a coin*

*and answer the appropriate question below.*

HEADS: *What was something encouraging*

*or positive that happened today?*

TAILS: *What was something disappointing*

*or difficult that happened today?*

Love Talks

FOR FAMILIES

*For* this love talk, each person will need a paper or

Styrofoam cup. Each person is to craft

(that is, draw, color, cut, tear, poke holes,

or attach objects to) his or her cup

in order to illustrate one of the following:

☐ *How I feel today or this week*

☐ *My spiritual life right now*

*F*or this love talk, each person will need a paper or

Styrofoam cup. Each person is to craft

(that is, draw, color, cut, tear, poke holes,

or attach objects to) his or her cup

in order to illustrate one of the following:

☐ *How I feel today or this week*

☐ *My spiritual life right now*

*L*ove *T*alks
FOR FAMILIES

*Pick one aroma that makes you say "Aaahhhh."*

☐ fresh brewed coffee ☐ fresh baked brownies

☐ new leather ☐ steaks broiling on a charcoal grill

☐ new car interior ☐ fresh baked bread

☐ honeysuckle in the breeze ☐ newly cut Christmas tree

*Now come up with an additional*

*favorite scent on your own.*

Love Talks
FOR FAMILIES

*Pick one aroma that makes you say "Aaahhhh."*

☐ *fresh brewed coffee*

☐ *new leather*

☐ *new car interior*

☐ *honeysuckle in the breeze*

☐ *fresh baked brownies*

☐ *steaks broiling on a charcoal grill*

☐ *fresh baked bread*

☐ *newly cut Christmas tree*

*Now come up with an additional*

*favorite scent on your own.*

Love Talks

FOR FAMILIES

*Complete this sentence: "I know you've heard me say it before, but I just want to tell you again: . . ." (Be original; say something other than "I love you.")*

Love Talks

FOR FAMILIES

*Complete this sentence: "I know you've heard me say it before, but I just want to tell you again: . . ." (Be original; say something other than "I love you.")*

Love Talks
FOR FAMILIES

*If our house were on fire and everyone (including pets) was safe outside and you could safely retrieve one personal item, what would it be?*

Love Talks
FOR FAMILIES

*If our house were on fire and everyone (including pets) was safe outside and you could safely retrieve one personal item, what would it be?*

Love Talks

FOR FAMILIES

*Congratulations! You just foiled a robbery at one of your favorite stores. To say thanks, the manager has promised you a lifetime 50 percent discount. In what store will you be enjoying this savings?*

Love Talks

FOR FAMILIES

*Congratulations! You just foiled a robbery at one of your favorite stores. To say thanks, the manager has promised you a lifetime 50 percent discount. In what store will you be enjoying this savings?*

Love Talks
FOR FAMILIES

*Who is one of your favorite fictional characters?*
*(This character may be from a book,*
*short story, movie, video, television show,*
*Saturday cartoon, comic book, or comic strip.)*

Love Talks
FOR FAMILIES

*Who is one of your favorite fictional characters?*
*(This character may be from a book,*
*short story, movie, video, television show,*
*Saturday cartoon, comic book, or comic strip.)*

# *What is one of your favorite sounds?*

☐ a steady rain at night when I am in bed

☐ crickets chirping

☐ ocean waves through the open window

☐ coffee brewing in the morning

☐ a ringing phone, knowing it's for me

☐ the bell signaling school is dismissed

☐ an ice cream truck chiming on the street

☐ children laughing

☐ my favorite music

☐ other _____

Love Talks
FOR FAMILIES

# *What is one of your favorite sounds?*

☐ *a steady rain at night when I am in bed*

☐ *crickets chirping*

☐ *ocean waves through the open window*

☐ *coffee brewing in the morning*

☐ *a ringing phone, knowing it's for me*

☐ *the bell signaling school is dismissed*

☐ *an ice cream truck chiming on the street*

☐ *children laughing*

☐ *my favorite music*

☐ *other* _____

*Your family is burying a time capsule
that will be opened one hundred years from now.
What two items will each of you place in
the capsule that illustrate something
about your life right now?*

Love Talks
FOR FAMILIES

*Your* family is burying a time capsule

that will be opened one hundred years from now.

What two items will each of you place in

the capsule that illustrate something

about your life right now?

*Love Talks*

FOR FAMILIES

*If you could travel in the future to any time*

*in your life to find out what happens*

*or just to enjoy the moment, what period or moment*

*in your life would you want to observe and why?*

*Love Talks*

FOR FAMILIES

*If you could travel in the future to any time*

*in your life to find out what happens*

*or just to enjoy the moment, what period or moment*

*in your life would you want to observe and why?*

Love Talks
FOR FAMILIES

*In the National Hockey League, the team that wins the championship receives a large trophy called the Stanley Cup. It is tradition that each member of the championship team enjoy personal possession of the Stanley Cup for a day. If you could take possession of anything in the world for one day, what would you choose?*

Love Talks
FOR FAMILIES

*In the National Hockey League, the team that wins the championship receives a large trophy called the Stanley Cup. It is tradition that each member of the championship team enjoy personal possession of the Stanley Cup for a day. If you could take possession of anything in the world for one day, what would you choose?*

Love Talks
FOR FAMILIES

## *If you were a country, which would you be?*

☐ *Australia—mysterious and wild*

☐ *Israel—small but mighty*

☐ *Bahamas—warm and friendly*

☐ *United States—proud and ambitious*

☐ *Italy—inspiring*

☐ *Canada—big but gentle*

☐ *Japan—small but resourceful*

☐ *England—traditional*

☐ *Russia—dealing with changes and challenges*

☐ *France—elegant*

# *If you were a country, which would you be?*

☐ *Australia—mysterious and wild*

☐ *Israel—small but mighty*

☐ *Bahamas—warm and friendly*

☐ *United States—proud and ambitious*

☐ *Italy—inspiring*

☐ *Canada—big but gentle*

☐ *Japan—small but resourceful*

☐ *England—traditional*

☐ *Russia—dealing with changes and challenges*

☐ *France—elegant*

*The U.S. Postal Service has said that if you'll agree to be a mail carrier for the summer while some of their workers take vacation, they will provide you with the vehicle of your choice for your postal route. What's your choice of vehicle?*

*T*he U.S. Postal Service has said that if you'll agree

to be a mail carrier for the summer while some

of their workers take vacation, they will provide

you with the vehicle of your choice for your postal

route. What's your choice of vehicle?

Love Talks
FOR FAMILIES

*Which of the Seven Dwarfs are you today— Bashful, Dopey, Sleepy, Sneezy, Grumpy, Happy, or Doc?*

*Which of the Seven Dwarfs are you today—
Bashful, Dopey, Sleepy, Sneezy, Grumpy,
Happy, or Doc?*

Love Talks
FOR FAMILIES

$C$HILDREN: *What toy or activity most engages your imagination or concentration?*

PARENTS: *As a child or teen, what toy or activity most engaged your imagination or concentration? What pleasant activity most engages it now?*

$L$ove $T$alks
FOR FAMILIES

*C*HILDREN: *What toy or activity most engages*

*your imagination or concentration?*

PARENTS: *As a child or teen, what toy or activity most*

*engaged your imagination or concentration?*

*What pleasant activity most engages it now?*

– QUESTION 89 –

*What product, service, place, or event are you so enthusiastic about that you'd make a good salesperson or spokesperson for it?*

*Love Talks*
FOR FAMILIES

*What product, service, place, or event are you so enthusiastic about that you'd make a good salesperson or spokesperson for it?*

*Something I'm looking forward to*

*in the next few weeks or months is . . .*

Love Talks
FOR FAMILIES

*Something I'm looking forward to
in the next few weeks or months is . . .*

Love Talks
FOR FAMILIES

*What do you think you would have said*
*if Jesus had chosen you to be one of his*
*twelve disciples? Recall a time that it felt good*
*to be chosen by a person, group, team, or committee.*

Love Talks
FOR FAMILIES

— QUESTION 91 —

*What do you think you would have said if Jesus had chosen you to be one of his twelve disciples? Recall a time that it felt good to be chosen by a person, group, team, or committee.*

Love Talks

FOR FAMILIES

*Recall a time when you were either not chosen*

*for something or by someone.*

*When was it? How did you feel?*

Love Talks

FOR FAMILIES

*Recall a time when you were either not chosen*

*for something or by someone.*

*When was it? How did you feel?*

Love Talks

FOR FAMILIES

*In Luke 17 ten lepers were healed of their disease, but only one returned to thank Jesus. Think of something that each family member has done for you recently. Then express your thanks by saying, "I really appreciated it when you . . ." or "Thank you for . . ."*

Love Talks

FOR FAMILIES

*In Luke 17 ten lepers were healed of their disease,
but only one returned to thank Jesus. Think of something
that each family member has done for you recently.
Then express your thanks by saying, "I really appreciated
it when you . . ." or "Thank you for . . ."*

Love Talks
FOR FAMILIES

*If you could ask Jesus to further explain*

*something He said or did as recorded in*

*the New Testament, what would you ask Him about?*

*If you could ask Jesus to further explain*

*something He said or did as recorded in*

*the New Testament, what would you ask Him about?*

Love Talks

FOR FAMILIES

– QUESTION 95 –

*W*ho is perhaps the best teacher
you've ever had? Explain your choice.

Love Talks
FOR FAMILIES

*Who is perhaps the best teacher
you've ever had? Explain your choice.*

*Love Talks*
FOR FAMILIES

CHILDREN: *What is something you remember*
*about a time you were very sick or injured?*

PARENTS: *What is something you remember*
*about your children's illnesses or injuries?*

Love Talks
FOR FAMILIES

*C*HILDREN: *What is something you remember about a time you were very sick or injured?*

PARENTS: *What is something you remember about your children's illnesses or injuries?*

*L*ove *T*alks
FOR FAMILIES

*Sometimes I wish I were more like*

*(someone you know), because . . .*

*Sometimes I wish I were more like*

*(someone you know), because . . .*

Love Talks
FOR FAMILIES

*P*ick any room in your home. Using your imagination, how would you like to remodel, redecorate, and/or furnish the room?

Love Talks

FOR FAMILIES

*Pick any room in your home. Using your imagination, how would you like to remodel, redecorate, and/or furnish the room?*

*Love Talks*
FOR FAMILIES

*Describe the perfect Saturday.*

*Describe the perfect Saturday.*

Love Talks
FOR FAMILIES

$\mathcal{W}$ho is one of your favorite people in our church?

$\mathcal{L}$ove $\mathcal{T}$alks
FOR FAMILIES

*Who is one of your favorite people in our church?*

*Before answering this last question you will want to give family members a chance to skim through the previous questions.*

PARENTS: *Recall one of your child's responses that was especially interesting and meaningful to you. Tell everyone which one it was and why.*

CHILDREN: *Recall one of the responses your parents gave to a question. Tell everyone which one it was and why.*

Love Talks
FOR FAMILIES

*B*efore answering this last question you will want to give family members

a chance to skim through the previous questions.

PARENTS: *Recall one of your child's responses that was*

*especially interesting and meaningful to you. Tell everyone*

*which one it was and why.*

CHILDREN: *Recall one of the responses your parents gave*

*to a question. Tell everyone which one it was and why.*

Love Talks

FOR FAMILIES